MATERIALS THAT MATTER

TEXTILES

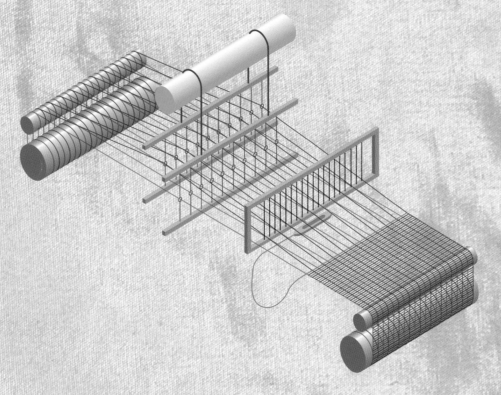

Neil Morris

amicus

Published by Amicus
P.O. Box 1329
Mankato, MN 56002

Printed in the United States of America,
at Corporate Graphics, North Mankato, Minnesota.

Library of Congress Cataloging-in-Publication Data
Morris, Neil.
  Textiles / by Neil Morris.
    p. cm. -- (Materials that matter)
  Summary: "Discusses textiles as a material, including historical uses, current uses, manufacturing, and recycling"--Provided by publisher.
  Includes bibliographical references and index.
  ISBN 978-1-60753-069-5 (lib. bdg.)
  1. Textile fabrics--Juvenile literature. I. Title.
  TS1446.M67 2011
  677--dc22
                                          2009051434

Created by Appleseed Editions Ltd.
Designed by Helen James
Edited by Mary-Jane Wilkins
Artwork by Graham Rosewarne
Picture research by Su Alexander

Photograph acknowledgements
page 4 Dennis Marsico/Corbis; 5 Xu Congjun/Xinhua Press/Corbis; 6 The Petrie Museum; 7 Philipus/Alamy; 8 Michael Nicholson/Corbis; 9 World History Archive/Alamy; 10 Philip Gould/Corbis; 11 Richard Hamilton Smith/Corbis; 12 Albrecht G Schaefer/Corbis; 13 George Brice/Alamy; 14 Fritz Polking; Frank Lane Picture Agency/Corbis; 15 Carl & Ann Purcell/Corbis; 16 Eric K K /Corbis; 17 Peter Bowater/Alamy; 18 David Butow/Corbis SABA; 20 & 21 Michael Rosenfeld/Science Faction/Corbis; 22 Stringer Shanghai/Reuters/Corbis; 23 Vittoriano Rastelli/Corbis; 24 The London Art Archive/Alamy; 25 Catherine Karnow/Corbis; 26 Coolangie/Alamy; 27 Alain Nogues/Sygma/Corbis; 28 Wu Wei/Xinhua Press/Corbis; 29 Sion Touhig/Corbis
Front cover Michael Rosenfeld/Science Faction/Corbis

DAD0041
32010

9 8 7 6 5 4 3 2 1

Contents

What Are Textiles?

Textiles are woven fabrics or cloths. The word "textile" comes from the Latin word for woven. A textile can be any kind of cloth. We make some by hand, but most are made in factories. Our clothes are made of textiles, and goods such as blankets, curtains, and towels are also made from textiles.

Textiles come in every color. In this shop in Italy, different fabrics and colors are stacked right up to the ceiling.

Natural Fibers

Textiles are made from **fibers** or **filaments**, which are thin threads of material. Many natural fibers come from plants, such as cotton, **flax**, and **jute**. Cotton fibers make a fabric that we also call cotton. Flax fibers make a cloth called linen. We make clothes and household goods from both. Jute fibers come from tree bark, and they make sacks and rope. Two well-known textiles come from animal fibers. One is wool from sheep. The other is silk, a fine fiber made by the caterpillars of an Asian moth.

Spinning into Yarn

Most natural fibers are too short to form a long thread. Individual cotton fibers, for example, are just about 1 inch (2.5 cm) long. So we spin them together, to make them longer and stronger. Spinners used to do this by hand, but today machines do most of the work. The twisted strand of fibers is called **yarn**.

Weaving Yarns

To make fabric, textile workers weave yarns together on a **loom** (see pages 18–19). Weavers once operated their looms by hand, and some still do. But today most cloth is woven on power-driven looms in factories. The loom joins sets of yarns together and weaves in patterns and designs.

PLASTIC THREADS

Some modern textiles are made with **man-made** fibers (see pages 16–17). Scientists first produced these by mixing chemicals together. Many of the chemicals come originally from petroleum. They are turned into a kind of runny plastic, which can produce long, thin threads called filaments. Acrylic, nylon, and polyester are all man-made fibers.

REUSING TEXTILES

We can reuse or recycle many textiles (see pages 26–27). Many people give unwanted or outgrown clothes to thrift stores or sell them in garage sales. Charities send clothes to people in developing countries. Poor-quality fabrics can be pulled apart and used to make wiping rags, furniture, padding, and other products.

Recycling helps the environment in many ways, reducing:
- the quantity of **raw materials** used, such as cotton or wool;
- the amount of water used;
- the amount of **carbon dioxide** and other polluting gases the industry emits;
- waste dumped into landfills.

Workers check the machines in a textile factory in China. Today, all the spinning is done automatically.

Early Textiles

Textiles do not last as long as materials such as metal. **Archaeologists** determine how people used textiles years ago by studying small pieces of fabric they have found, as well as needles and other tools. Old drawings and sculptures also show that people sewed and wove textiles more than 20,000 years ago.

In Ancient Times

Twisted plant fibers found in present-day Israel show that people were making cord for nets and bags thousands of years ago. At another site, experts found pieces of linen clothing that date back to 8000 BC. Similar finds have been made in ancient Mesopotamia (modern Iraq) and Turkey, and archaeologists have also found woolen clothes from that time. Later, the ancient Egyptians became skillful at weaving linen. They were known throughout the ancient world for their fine, colorful clothing.

Tunics of Linen and Wool

The ancient Greeks used woolen textiles for clothes, although they also liked linen. Both men and women wore a long tunic called a "chiton." The Romans wore a similar tunic, called a "toga," which was made of heavy, white wool. Both men and women originally wore this, but the toga gradually became a garment only men wore. Women continued to wear a simple tunic, with a long, full dress over it. The pleated dress was called a "stola."

This linen tunic was found in an ancient Egyptian tomb. It is more than 4,000 years old.

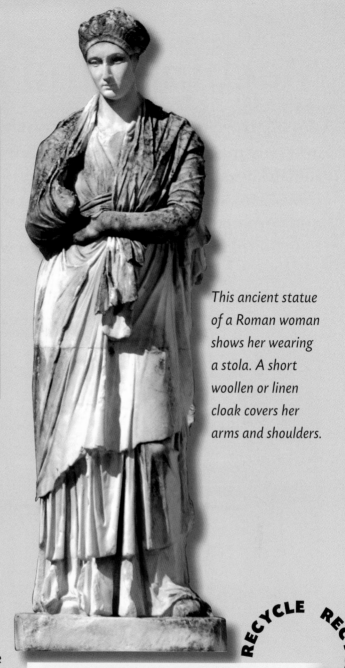

This ancient statue of a Roman woman shows her wearing a stola. A short woollen or linen cloak covers her arms and shoulders.

Spindles and Spinning Wheels

In ancient times, people used a handheld rod, called a **spindle**, to spin fibers into thread. The invention of the spinning wheel made spinning easier and faster. Spinners in India probably used the first wheel around 500 BC.

About 2,000 years later, spinners in Saxony (modern Germany) added a **treadle** to make things easier. By then weavers had been using a simple loom for hundreds of years. Before the **Industrial Revolution** (see pages 8–9), people made textiles at home. The whole family would work together in this **cottage industry**. Merchants gave families spinning wheels and looms. They also provided them with raw materials, such as wool, and collected the fabrics when they were ready.

RECYCLE RECYCLE RECYCLE RECYCLE

Machines and Inventions

During the eighteenth century, amazing inventions and new machines completely changed the way textiles were made. This was the time of the Industrial Revolution, which began in Britain and spread to the rest of Europe and North America. New factories made spinning and weaving much faster.

Nineteenth-century power looms changed the textile industry. This one made a heavy white cotton cloth.

Powering Up

At first, waterwheels powered the machines, then steam power took over. By the end of the century, textile mills mass-produced clothes and other goods for many people. In just over 50 years, several inventions revolutionized the textile industry. The first was the flying **shuttle** in 1733, which wove yarns together mechanically rather than by hand. Then came three improved water-powered spinning machines. They were followed by the first power loom, which was driven by water or steam. By 1833, there were 100,000 power looms in Britain.

The spinning jenny could spin 16 yarns at a time. The spinner operated the machine by hand.

Chance Discovery?

Some historians believe that the idea behind the **spinning jenny** was the result of an accident. The story goes that one day the English weaver James Hargreaves was watching his daughter at her spinning wheel at home. When she stood up, the wheel tipped over and continued to turn on the floor. This gave Hargreaves the idea for upright spindles, which he placed in a row in a frame. This was the first device to wind yarn onto more than one spindle at a time. Hargreaves may have named his machine a jenny after his daughter.

FROM THE UK TO THE U.S.

During the 1700s, British businessmen tried to keep their inventions secret. Cotton was exported from America to be spun and woven into textiles in England. The British government did not allow anyone who knew about the new spinning machines to leave the country. They feared that they would give secrets away. In 1789, English textile worker Samuel Slater (1768–1835) sailed to America and set up a spinning factory in Rhode Island. Just four years later, the invention of the **cotton gin** revolutionized the cotton industry by speeding up production (see page 11).

Cotton for Comfort

More textiles are made of cotton than any other natural fiber. It is ideal for clothes, as it wicks away moisture from the wearer's skin. Cotton clothes feel warm in winter and cool in summer. More than 25 million tons (23 million t) of raw cotton are produced every year. China, India, and the U.S. grow more than two-thirds of this among them.

Growing and Picking

There are different kinds of cotton plants, and they all grow best in warm parts of the world. One, called tree cotton, first grew in India. Another, called upland cotton, originated in Central America and is now the most common variety in the world.

Cotton fibers grow around the plant's seeds inside a round seed pod called a "**boll**." When the plant ripens, the boll splits open, and it is time to harvest the fibers and seeds. Cotton pickers once did this by hand and still do in countries such as Uzbekistan. But in most places, machines pick cotton and collect the seeds and fibers. Different machines press this seed cotton into large stacks that can weigh up to 22,000 pounds (10,000 kg).

A cotton-picking machine harvests cotton in Louisiana.

TOP COTTON GROWERS

	Million Tons		
China	8.4	Pakistan	2.2
India	4.9	Brazil	1.5
USA	4.6		

Source: Food and Agriculture Organization of the United Nations, 2007

A modern gin in Mississippi produces much more cotton than old-fashioned methods.

THE FIRST COTTON GIN

It was hard work separating cotton fibers from seeds by hand. In 1793, American inventor Eli Whitney (1765–1825) came up with a machine that did this quickly and efficiently. He called it a cotton gin (short for engine). One machine did the work of 50 hand workers in the same time.

Powerful Machines

Today's cotton gins are large, powerful machines that do much more than Whitney's original version. Spinning saws pull the fibers through gaps that catch the seeds. Rotating brushes and blasts of air push the fibers together. They are then pressed into bales that weigh more than

USING THE SEEDS

The ginning process also separates the cotton seeds. Machines grind and press the seeds to produce cottonseed oil. This oil is used in margarine, cooking oils, and snack foods. One 496 pound (225 kg) bale of seeds produces enough oil to cook nearly 6,000 snack-sized bags of potato chips. Cottonseed oil can also be used in cosmetics and soap.

441 pounds (200 kg). The latest gins can produce as many as 60 bales of cotton fibers an hour. The fibers are then transported to a textile mill, where looms turn them into cotton fabric (see pages 18–19).

Wool for Warmth

Wool is mainly spun from the soft, curly hair of sheep, but some wool comes from other animals. Kashmir goats produce the fine, soft wool called "cashmere." Mohair is the silky wool of the Angora goat. Camels' hair is also called wool, as well as the coats of alpaca, llama, and vicuña, which come from South America.

Farmers all over the world keep sheep, and altogether more than a billion sheep produce over 2 million tons (1.8 million t) of wool every year. Between them, Australia and China produce nearly half the world's wool.

Top Wool Producers

Thousand Tons	
Australia	512.3
China	435.4
New Zealand	240.2
Iran	82.7
United Kingdom	68.3

Source: Food and Agriculture Organization of the United Nations, 2007

A skillful Australian sheepshearer removes a fleece.

Shearing Sheep

Wool is collected from sheep once a year, by shearing their fleeces. Skilled shearers use electric shears, which are like large hair clippers, to remove a sheep's fleece in one piece. A merino sheep produces about 8 to 11 pounds (4–5 kg) of wool every year.

From fleece to textile

Different parts of the fleece produce various qualities of wool, so the sheared wool is sorted. The fibers are judged by their strength, length, fineness (or width), crimp

A worker loads wool into a knitting machine in Shanghai, China.

(or waviness), and color. The whiter the shade, the better the wool. First the wool is cleaned and washed, then it is **carded**. This means untangling and combing the fibers, by passing them through wire teeth on a roller. Then the fibers are spun into yarn. Wool yarn is knitted or woven by hand or machine. Hand knitters use two long needles to interlock the yarn and make woolen clothes. Experienced knitters follow patterns to make garments in different shapes and colors. In factories, knitting machines have replaced hand knitters.

TRAVELING MERINOS

Merino sheep have the finest, softest wool. The breed was first known in Spain, where farmers kept their wool a secret. Before the eighteenth century, anyone who exported merinos from Spain could be sentenced to death. Nevertheless, a few rams and ewes were taken to Britain in 1787, and 10 years later, the British sent 13 merinos to Australia. By 1801, Australia had more than 33,000 sheep, and today it has about 114 million, mostly merinos.

SHODDY RECYCLING

RECYCLE RECYCLE RECYCLE RECYCLE

Old woolen clothes can be pulled apart or shredded. The fibers are mixed with other clippings, new raw wool, or another fiber, such as cotton, and respun. The respinning process was first used in Yorkshire, in northern England, in the early 1800s. The recycled wool is lower quality than new varieties, and is called "shoddy."

Shiny Silk

Silk has a soft, glossy shine, which makes it a beautiful-looking textile. Silk is made by silkworms, which are not real worms but the larvae (or caterpillars) of a moth. Silk moths come from East Asia and, like other moths and butterflies, their larvae spin cocoons.

The cocoons form protective coverings for the caterpillars during the period in which they turn into adult moths. They are made of silk fibers, and farmers collect them to make the beautiful textile. This was first done in ancient China, which still produces more than half the world's raw silk today.

Legendary Beginnings

According to legend, a Chinese empress discovered silk about 2,700 years ago. Emperor Huangdi asked his wife, Leizu, to find out what was damaging the mulberry trees in his garden. The empress found small, white caterpillars eating the trees' leaves and spinning cocoons, and she collected a few to show the emperor. Later, while she was having tea, Leizu accidentally dropped a cocoon into hot water and was amazed to see a delicate thread come from it. She had discovered silk.

Each silkworm cocoon, about 0.8 inch (2 cm) across, contains hundreds of yards (meters) of raw silk.

TOP SILK PRODUCERS

	Thousand Tons
China	330.70
India	84.88
Uzbekistan	19.84
Brazil	9.04
Iran	6.61

Source: Food and Agriculture Organization of the United Nations, 2007

Producing Yarn

Silk farmers keep silkworm eggs on trays with mulberry leaves. When the caterpillars hatch, they eat the leaves. They grow bigger, until they are ready to change into **pupae** (or **chrysalises**) by spinning cocoons. When the cocoons are complete, the farmers steam or bake them, which kills the pupae.

The farmers leave a few cocoons to go on growing and turn into adult moths. They produce more eggs and continue the cycle. The harvested cocoons are loosened in hot water. Workers then unwind the silk filaments individually before winding them together on reels. They wind and twist several filaments together to make silk yarn.

Silk Farms and Wild Silk

The commercial breeding of silkworms is called "sericulture." Animal-rights groups are

REUSING WASTE

The beginnings and ends of each cocoon do not make high-quality thread. Also, caterpillars damage or even burst some cocoons. None of this silk is wasted. Farmers collect and spin the fibers into a lower-quality yarn known as "spun silk."

against sericulture and for the use of wild or artificial silk. Wild silk (or tussore) can be collected from different Asian moths that feed on oak leaves. The moths are allowed to develop and fly away before the cocoons are harvested. Tussore is less fine and shiny than cultivated silk. The organization People for the Ethical Treatment of Animals (PETA) believes that this a humane alternative to sericulture.

A silk-spinning machine in China.

Artificial Fibers

During the 1800s, scientists tried to create a man-made fiber. They wanted to develop an artificial silk that was cheaper to produce than natural silk. The scientists started with fibers from cellulose, which comes from the cell walls of wood and other plants.

They mixed the cellulose fibers with chemicals and formed a plastic **resin** that could be turned into long fibers. In the 1890s, this new material was called art (for artificial) silk, viscose, or rayon.

French Discoveries

During the 1860s, a disease that killed silkworms damaged the French silk industry. Chemist Louis Pasteur (1822–1895) discovered that a microbe had caused the problem. One of Pasteur's assistants, Hilaire Chardonnet (1839–1924), went on to study cellulose. One day, he spilled a bottle of a substance called "nitrocellulose" that he had made by mixing chemicals with a pulp of mulberry leaves (silkworms' food). Chardonnet saw that the liquid formed long, thin strands like silk. Encouraged, he worked further on the idea of artificial silk. In 1889, he showed his invention at the Paris Exhibition.

Researchers such as this chemist in Taiwan are always looking for new ways to make artificial fibers.

Spun Plastic

Artificial fibers are spun plastic. They were originally made from cellulose, and later plastic resin was made from chemicals alone. Most of the chemicals used to make plastic come from petroleum (crude oil), and they are turned into plastic resin, using great heat and pressure. To make filaments,

the hot, runny resin is forced through tiny holes in a plate called a "spinneret." As the fibers squirt out of the tiny holes, air is blasted at them to cool and harden them quickly. They are then stretched and wound onto **spools**.

Nylon Numbers

When nylon stockings first went on sale in American stores in 1939, they cost just one dollar a pair, and five million pairs were sold on the first day. Customers lined up to buy them, and they soon replaced expensive silk stockings.

Manufacturers needed a way of measuring the fineness of different nylon fibers. They used a unit called **denier**. A denier is the weight in grams of 9,843 yards (9,000 m) of yarn. So if that amount of nylon weighed 0.5 ounce (15 g), it was called 15-denier yarn. Today we use another unit, the tex, which is based on the weight of 1,094 yards (1,000 m) of yarn.

New Carpets for Old

RECYCLE RECYCLE RECYCLE RECYCLE

Nylon is used for making carpets, and old carpets can be recycled. The plastic fibers are melted down and added to a new plastic resin of the same type. The resin is turned into nylon fiber and woven into new carpets or other products.

Spinning and Weaving Yarn

Spinning machines stretch and twist fibers together to make yarn (see page 5). The yarns are then woven together to make fabrics, or cloth. Wool is also knitted (see page 13). Weavers and knitters use different patterns to create various effects, but the basic procedure is the same.

A worker checks a modern circular loom at a clothing factory in Mexico.

Blending Fibers

First the fibers are stretched and twisted together loosely, to make a slack thread called "rove" or "roving." Then they are stretched again, before being spun together to make yarn, and collected on a **bobbin** (or spool). Years ago, different fibers were spun individually, but today different materials are often spun together. The raw materials can be natural or artificial fibers, or a mixture of both. Manufacturers keep a careful note of their blends, and these usually appear on labels. For example, on the label of a sweater, you might find: 42% linen, 36% cotton, 22% nylon.

How a Loom Works

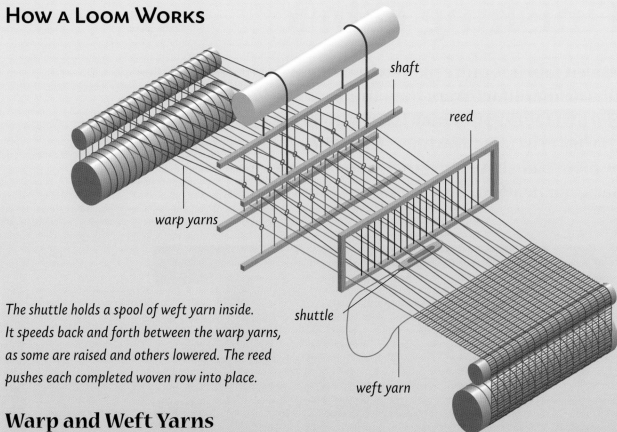

shaft

reed

warp yarns

shuttle

weft yarn

The shuttle holds a spool of weft yarn inside. It speeds back and forth between the warp yarns, as some are raised and others lowered. The reed pushes each completed woven row into place.

Warp and Weft Yarns

Two sets of yarns are woven together to make a piece of fabric. One set, called the **warp**, runs lengthwise. The other set, called the **weft**, runs widthwise. Warp and weft are woven on a loom. Weavers once operated looms by hand, but today most weaving is done in textile factories, using power looms. These are huge, powerful machines that work very fast.

The Weaving Process

On the loom, the weft yarns are threaded over and under the warp yarns. To do this, shafts on the loom alternately raise and lower some of the warp yarns. As this happens, a small cylindrical device called a "shuttle" passes the weft yarn between gaps in the warp. The gaps are there because the shafts alternately raise different warp yarns. The order in which this happens can be changed to make different kinds of weave.

Types of Weave

There are three basic weaves.
Plain weave is the most common. In the first row, the weft yarn passes under the first warp, over the second, and so on.
In the second row, it goes over the first warp, and so on.
Twill weave, in which the weft yarn passes over and then under two warps at a time. This creates a stronger fabric.
Satin weave, in which the weft yarn passes over four warps at a time, and then under one. This makes a smoother surface.

Finishing Fabric

Woven fabric is quite plain when it leaves the loom. Textile manufacturers then improve the look and feel of a fabric. They may treat it to bring out the best characteristics of the fiber. Then they might dye it or print a design on it. Finally, they iron the fabric between heavy rollers to make it flat and even.

Large bolts of fabric go though several processes in this textile plant. They receive a special finish and are dyed different colors.

Improving the Cloth

The finished fabric is wound onto **bolts**. These are rolls of fabric which are often 33 to 44 yards (30–40 m) long.

When fabrics leave the loom or knitting machine, they are known as "gray goods." Manufacturers use chemicals to bleach some gray goods, such as linen, to make them white. Various methods are used to add different finishes to fabrics. Cotton may be "mercerized." This means treating the fabric (or sometimes the yarn before it is woven) with caustic soda, making it stronger and shinier. Other fabrics, such as woollens, silks, and rayons, may be napped. They are passed over revolving rollers with fine wires that lift the fibers and give the fabric a soft surface.

Dyeing

Textiles can be dyed at any stage, from fibers to yarn and finished fabrics. Different colored yarns are woven to create stripes or other patterns, but most textiles are dyed when the fabric is complete.

Machines pull the fabric through a bath containing the dye, where heat and pressure are used to make the color strong and lasting. The **pigments** (or colors) are made from various chemical and organic substances.

Roller and Screen Printing

There are several ways of printing designs on finished fabrics. Textile manufacturers often use a method that is similar to printing on paper. A machine with large rollers transfers designs that have been engraved on the surface of the rollers. Each color ink or dye has a separate printing roller. Another common method uses a screen, which is like a stencil or mask. Dye or ink passes onto the fabric through a pattern on the screen, one color at a time. The different colors—usually four—work together to make up the finished pattern.

Workers check the quality of patterns at a textile printing plant in Germany.

Clothing and Fashion

The clothes we wear are made from textiles. Clothing companies buy large rolls of cloth (or bolts) from textile manufacturers. They make these up into clothes and sell them to stores. There customers choose the clothes they like to wear, find the right sizes, try them on, and buy them.

Making Clothes

Many people and processes are involved in turning textiles into clothes. During the first stage, mechanized knives and cutting machines cut the bolts of cloth into large, flat pieces. Skilled cutters then make smaller pieces of different shapes, following patterns created by a designer. Once the cutting out is completed, the clothes are sewn. Machinists sew different fabric pieces together, and special machines add finishes such as collars and cuffs. The finished garment is pressed and checked before it is delivered to the store.

Fashion Design

Fashion designers set the trends for new clothing styles. Top designers create unique dresses and other clothes for rich customers. Models show these creations at fashion

Chinese workers sew pieces of fabric together to make sweaters.

shows in London, Milan, New York, and Paris. Designer clothes are very expensive to buy. The top fashion items are usually made of expensive fabrics, such as silk. Stores keep their eye on the trends, and their designers produce ready-to-wear clothes in all sorts of different sizes and colors. These are more likely to be made of less expensive fabrics, such as cotton.

Fake Fur

Styles can go completely out of fashion. Once fur coats were fashionable during the winter, but recently many people have decided that they do not want to wear animal skins. They feel it is wrong to kill animals such as leopards for their pelts. These beliefs have led manufacturers to develop a new textile, known as fake or false fur. The material is made of **synthetic** fibers and can look like the real fur of animals, ranging from beaver to leopard or mink. In fact, the fakes have become so real looking that models wearing them have occasionally been accused of cruelty to animals.

CHANGING FASHIONS

Fashions change regularly, so there are new styles in the stores every season. This means people often throw away clothes before they are worn out. The clothing industry always has plenty of customers and so provides a lot of jobs. When people no longer want old clothes, many give them to thrift stores or recycle them.

23

Arts and Crafts

Throughout history, people have used textiles in art. Tapestries and wall hangings were popular during the Middle Ages in Europe. They were woven from different materials and helped keep out drafts, as well as brightening up walls. They might also tell a story, such as a traditional legend.

The Craft of William Morris

The English poet and designer William Morris (1834–96) was a skilled craftsman. He believed that the Industrial Revolution (see page 8) made artists forget how to make things by hand. Morris and his colleagues wanted people to value materials more. In 1861, Morris founded his own company, and he went on to create the **Arts and Crafts Movement** with other artists. He often worked with textiles and made beautiful carpets, wall hangings, and furniture. Artists who belonged to the movement believed that homes should be full of objects that were both practical and beautiful.

This woven tapestry was handmade in the Loire region of France, around 1510.

A Navajo woman weaves a rug in traditional style on a simple upright loom.

Furnishings

Textiles have always been used to cover chairs and sofas, as **upholstery**. William Morris designed upholstery, and twentieth-century artists carried on this tradition. One of the most famous is the U.S. textile designer Jack Lenor Larsen (born 1927), who studied ancient South American fabrics. Like Morris, Larsen has had great influence on other businesses, for example, designing upholstery for airlines.

Native American Traditions

Many Native American tribes are famous for their traditional textiles. In the villages of the southwest, the ancestors of the Navajo people used to spin, dye, and weave cotton. When the Spanish brought sheep to North America, the Navajo made blankets from their wool. They used hand looms to weave brilliant geometric patterns. Mothers passed this skill on to their daughters, and many modern Native Americans still weave.

Carpets from Asia

Countries throughout Asia have a long tradition of making oriental carpets or rugs, from the Caucasian mountains in the west to China in the east. The most famous are Persian carpets, from the region where Iran is today. Weavers make them by hand on simple looms, mainly using wool. Some original techniques are still kept secret by weavers. Patterns include trees, flowers, and geometric designs. The different types of Persian weaving are known as "knots," and they make fine rugs.

Recycling Textiles

We all throw away clothes, when they are no longer fashionable or the right size. If we put these textiles in the normal trash cans, they go to landfills to be dumped. Today we can reuse or recycle unwanted textiles, so that we use fewer raw materials and less energy to make new textiles.

Many cities have recycling drop-off sites for textiles. They collect used textiles along with other recycled items, such as glass and paper. Charities and their stores also resell donated clothes and other textiles.

Sorting for Recycling

Recycling units start by sorting the textiles. Good-quality clothing may be given to charity or sent to developing countries. Other textiles in good condition can be rewoven. This means pulling the threads apart, blending them with new fibers, and weaving them into new fabrics. Worn and damaged items can be cleaned and reprocessed into industrial wiping rags, roofing felt, or furniture padding.

Taking Clothing Back

Some clothing companies, such as those that sell specialized sportswear made of artificial fibers, run their own recycling operation.

Customers can return their used clothing to the company, by mail or through one of their stores.

Remelting Plastics

Fabrics made of artificial fibers can be reused in the same way as nylon carpet (see page 17). Machines cut the garments

Textile drop-off sites are a useful and easy way to recycle unwanted clothes.

Clothes are sorted into different types at a recycling center in France.

into small pieces, which are ground down into tiny plastic pellets. The pellets can be re-melted and spun into filaments, ready to be turned into new artificial fabrics.

Patchwork

The craft of patchwork or quilting is a good way to reuse scraps of fabric. Quilters sew the scraps—or patches—together to make a quilt, or cover. This is a traditional craft, and it became popular in North America during the eighteenth century, when settlers found that cloth was scarce. They started cutting old clothes and bed linen into strips and patches, and pieced them together into patterns. The patterns were a combination of shapes—squares, triangles, and diamonds. The craft is still popular today.

RECYCLE RECYCLE RECYCLE RECYCLE

RAG AND BONE MEN

In the past, rag and bone men collected unwanted textiles, roast joint bones, scrap iron, and other unwanted items. They traveled the streets with a horse and cart, shouting "Rags and bones!" and people brought them their unwanted items. They were the first recyclers and sold rags to textile merchants or papermakers. During the 1700s and 1800s, papermakers often used cotton and linen rags to make pulp for paper. The bones were mainly used to make glue.

Textiles in the Future

How will natural fibers change in the future? Scientists may find new plants and animals to provide fibers and new ways to spin and weave. Scientists are working on artificial fibers that are stronger than nylon and other synthetic fibers. Many clothing buyers still prefer traditional textiles, such as silk and cotton.

Athletes such as the champion sprinter Usain Bolt (center), race in light, streamlined fabrics.

Modern Microfibers

Modern thin fibers, called microfibers, have been used to make new kinds of textiles in recent years. Lycra is a stretchy fiber that is ideal for sportswear. GORE-TEX is a fabric that allows moisture to pass through one way only. So it keeps rain out but lets sweat through. Scientists are constantly working on new microfibers, to make more practical textiles. They will continue to create new synthetic fibers that will be even stretchier, lighter, or more waterproof—or perhaps they will come up with one fiber which has all these qualities.

Textiles and Health

Modern textiles are used in hospitals to make antiseptic bandages and supports. Artificial fibers have also been invented that the human body will not reject. This means that these biotextiles can be used to make artificial blood vessels, heart valves, and even shock absorbers in the spine. Medical researchers are working on more new biotextiles that will help future surgeons.

Changing Genes

Wouldn't it be amazing if cotton farmers could grow crops in different colors? Or if sheep farmers could produce longer wool? This might be possible in the future. Scientists already know how to change some characteristics of plants and animals by altering their **genes**. All plants and animals have biological sets of instructions within their cells. These are carried by genes, which pass the code on to the next generation.

So it could be possible to change a crop's color or an animal's coat. Many environmentalists are against such **genetic modification** (or GM for short). They say that GM crops are unnatural and may turn out to be dangerous to both the environment and human health in the long term. They believe that GM crops could spread, wiping out natural plants and reducing the variety of plants and animals.

Recycling More

People are recycling more glass, paper, plastic, and textiles than ever before. As we all become more aware of waste and the problems of dumping waste in landfills, we will reuse and recycle more and more textiles. New ways may be found to take fabrics apart quickly and cheaply, so that the fibers can be reused. Who knows, your old sweaters might become a new felt tent for a herding family in Mongolia!

Protesters try to destroy GM crops in test fields in England.

Glossary

archaeologist   A person who studies the past by digging up and studying remains.

Arts and Crafts Movement   A group of English artists in the 1800s who raised standards of craftsmanship.

bobbin   A cylinder on which yarn is wound; a spool or reel.

boll   The seed pod of a cotton plant.

bolt   A large roll of fabric.

carbon dioxide (CO_2)   A greenhouse gas given off when we burn fossil fuels, such as coal, oil, and gas.

card   To untangle and comb fibers of wool or cotton.

cellulose   A substance that makes up the cell walls of plants.

chrysalis   An insect inside a cocoon which is changing from a larva to an adult; also called pupa.

cocoon   The covering made by a larva when it becomes a chrysalis, before turning into an adult insect.

cottage industry   A small business based in a home rather than in a factory.

cotton gin   A machine that separates cotton from its seeds.

denier   A unit that measures the fineness of silk or nylon yarn.

fibers   Thin threads of material that come from plants or animals, or are made from plastic. Yarns and cloths made from these are also called fibers.

filament   A slender thread.

flax   A plant used to make linen.

gene   A tiny part of a living cell that controls the characteristics of a living thing and which is passed on to the next generation.

genetic modification (GM)   Using technology to change the genes of plants or animals and alter their characteristics.

Industrial Revolution   The rapid development of machinery, factories, and industry that began in the late 1700s.

jute   A tropical plant with tough fibers that are used to make sacks and rope.

larva (plural larvae)   Young wormlike insects; also called caterpillar or grub.

loom   A machine for weaving thread or yarn into cloth.

man-made fiber   Thin threads of material made from plastics, such as nylon.

mulberry   A kind of tree. Silkworms eat its leaves.

pigment   A substance that gives a material color.

pupa   See chrysalis.

raw material   A natural material, such as cotton, before it is processed and used to make something.

resin   Basic plastic material before it is spun into a man-made fiber.

shuttle   A weaving device that holds thread and passes it through a loom.

Silk Road   An ancient trade route from China to Europe; merchants carried silk along the route.

spindle   A handheld rod used in ancient times to spin fibers into thread and later used in spinning machines.

spinning jenny   A machine that wound yarn onto several spindles at once.

spool   A cylinder for winding yarn. Also called a bobbin or reel.

synthetic   Made artificially, rather than from natural materials.

treadle   A flat pedal pushed up and down by the operator's feet to work a machine.

upholstery   The fabric and stuffing used to cover chairs and other furniture.

warp   The yarns that run lengthwise on a loom.

weft   The yarns that run widthwise on a loom.

yarn   A continuous twisted strand of fibers, such as cotton or wool; thread.

Web Sites

Information on textile recycling, including answers to "Why bother?"
http://www.epa.gov/waste/conserve/materials/textiles.htm

Story of cotton, from the plant to the finished material and its uses, by the National Cotton Council of America
http://www.cotton.org/pubs/cottoncounts/fieldtofabric/index.cfm

History of Clothing for Kids, with links to information about wool, silk, cotton, and other textile materials.
http://www.historyforkids.org/learn/clothing/wool.htm

Textiles and the materials used to make them, including detailed articles about natural and synthetic fibers.
http://www.fabrics.net/

A history of the U.S. textile industry.
http://inventors.about.com/od/indrevolution/a/history_textile.htm

Index